BEES!

A MY INCREDIBLE WORLD PICTURE BOOK

MY INCREDIBLE WORLD

Copyright © 2021, My Incredible World

All rights reserved. This book or any portion thereof may not be reproduced or used in any manner whatsoever without the express written permission of the copyright holder.

www.myincredibleworld.com

Photo Credits:
Cover. David Clode, https://unsplash.com/photos/wRt8myE0W00
Page 1. Dmitry Grigoriev, https://unsplash.com/photos/yxXpjF-RmA
Page 2. Jason Leung, https://unsplash.com/photos/Qgb9urMZ8lw
Page 3. Kelsey Krajewski, https://unsplash.com/photos/hGA9eOkhjAQ
Page 4. Ingemar Johnsson, https://unsplash.com/photos/rMD5tXL2pgE
Page 5. Dustin Humes, https://unsplash.com/photos/Xd-DRy9jJMc
Page 6. Rowan Heuvel, https://unsplash.com/photos/mHaGFQPalxA
Page 7. Edgar Chaparro, https://unsplash.com/photos/3bq0o08flG0
Page 8. Andy Holmes, https://unsplash.com/photos/wdz-dez94RQ
Page 9. Kianadali, https://unsplash.com/photos/XycDjxmA-nQ
Page 10. Erik Karits, https://unsplash.com/photos/VTHLVXYP6E0
Page 11. Damien Tupinier, https://unsplash.com/photos/IgNjT3VTPMc
Page 12. Stephen Bedase, https://unsplash.com/photos/CFnRv8RaphA
Page 13. Tania P., https://unsplash.com/photos/BM_31yfHkK0
Page 14. Shelby Cohron, https://unsplash.com/photos/UQwbKtu-2Ek
Page 15. Annie Spratt, https://unsplash.com/photos/XlTEP0u29L4
Page 16. Wolfgang Hasselm, https://unsplash.com/photos/Xd-DRy9jJMc
Page 17. Krzysztof Niewolny, https://unsplash.com/photos/0ndNO8ZiUgs
Page 18. Michelle Atkinson, https://unsplash.com/photos/aYgTkQRVUAk
Page 19. Boris Smokrovic, https://unsplash.com/photos/gr7ZkoZnHXU
Page 20. Stafano Ghezzi, https://unsplash.com/photos/dn2O-LZRdmE
Page 21. Milan Ivanovic, https://unsplash.com/photos/1lo77Df802I
Page 22. Leandro Fregoni, https://unsplash.com/photos/SLgbKHthfpA

Bees are found on every continent in the world except Antarctica!

There are more than 20,000 species of bees!

Bees are insects with 6 legs, 4 wings, and 5 eyes!

Bees are important because they are **pollinators** that help plants grow fruit and seeds.

They have a long tongue called a **proboscis** that helps them slurp up nectar from flowers!

Honeybees live in hives with other bees (called a **colony**).

There are 3 types of bees in each colony: the **queen**, **worker bees**, and **drones**.

The queen and worker bees are always female!

Drones are always male and don't collect pollen!

Only female bees have stingers, but many can't sting!

The queen bee is bigger than the others, and lays most, if not all, the eggs in a colony.

The life cycle of a bee has 4 stages: **egg**, **larva**, **pupa**, and **adult**.

It usually takes about 21 days for a honeybee egg to become an adult bee!

Only a small minority of bee species make honey.

Honeybees can be kept by humans to make honey!

It takes 500 to 600 bees to make one pound (.45 kg) of honey!

The smallest species of bees only grows to around 2 millimeters long!

The largest species can grow to almost 4 centimeters long!

Some bee species can fly as fast as 20 miles per hour (32 kph).

Bees can see all colors except for red.

They have an excellent sense of smell that is around 100 times more sensitive than humans!

Bees are incredible!